SECRETS

OF AMERICAN HISTORY

★ WORLD WAR I ★

Fearless Flyers, Dazzle Painters, and Code Talkers!

by Elizabeth Dennis

illustrated by Valerio Fabbretti

Ready-to-Read

Simon Spotlight
New York London Toronto Sydney New Delhi

SIMON SPOTLIGHT
An imprint of Simon & Schuster Children's Publishing Division
1230 Avenue of the Americas, New York, New York 10020
This Simon Spotlight edition December 2018
Text copyright © 2018 by Simon & Schuster, Inc.
Illustrations copyright © 2018 by Valerio Fabbretti
SIMON SPOTLIGHT, READY-TO-READ, and colophon are registered trademarks of Simon & Schuster, Inc.
For information about special discounts for bulk purchases, please contact Simon & Schuster Special Sales at
1-866-506-1949 or business@simonandschuster.com.
Manufactured in China 0918 SDI

Contents

Chapter 1
The Great War

What do you know about World War I? You might know that it started in 1914, but did you know that battleships were covered in "Razzle Dazzle" painting? And that a reporter said it made them look like floating Easter eggs? Or that American Indians from the Choctaw Nation helped win battles by talking on the telephone using the Choctaw language as a secret code?

World War I was also the first war that used airplanes, submarines, and other technologies that were new at the time. While these inventions caused a lot of destruction, they inspired people to find creative ways to defeat the enemy.

These new inventions provided job opportunities for people who didn't yet have equal rights in the United States. A group of talented women couldn't vote, but they contributed to the war effort while scaling the sides of huge ships. And a man named Eugene Bullard became the first African American fighter pilot.

Learn about their true stories and more in this book that unlocks the secrets of American history!

When World War I started, many countries were under the control of one of four large empires: Great Britain, Russia, Austria-Hungary, and Germany. These empires, and many other countries, had promised to protect one another in agreements called alliances (uh-LIE-en-says). If the country of Serbia was attacked, for example, its alliance with the Russian Empire meant that Russia would help defend Serbia.

The war began on June 28, 1914, when a Serbian man killed Archduke Franz Ferdinand and his wife. The archduke was next in line to become the emperor of Austria-Hungary, and the Serbian man was upset because Austria-Hungary had taken control of Bosnia. He wanted Serbia to control Bosnia instead. His actions set off the First World War.

As a response to the deaths, Austria-Hungary declared war on Serbia. Because of its alliance with Serbia, Russia joined the fight. Soon Germany, Great Britain, and many other countries joined too, each choosing a side in the largest war the world had ever seen.

One side was called the Central Powers and included Germany, Austria-Hungary, Bulgaria, and the Ottoman Empire. The other side was called the Allied Powers, or Allies, and included Great Britain, France, Italy, Russia, Romania, Japan, and eventually the United States, which joined in 1917.

This war lasted for four long years. It was also fought differently from previous wars. Before, many wars were fought in plain sight and at a close distance on battlefields. But World War I was fought from trenches dug out of the earth, from up in the sky in airplanes, and from underwater in submarines, with weapons that could hit a target from far away.

These changes made it necessary for people to find creative solutions to complicated problems and to do whatever they could to help end the war.

Chapter 2
Cubism, Camouflage, and Razzle Dazzle

One of the amazing things that came about during World War I was called Razzle Dazzle painting, and it helped keep ships afloat. How could *paint* keep a ship from sinking? Believe it or not, the answer has to do with zebra stripes and paintings by Pablo Picasso!

It all started because Germany's submarines, also called U-boats, were hitting Allied ships with torpedoes.

The Allies needed to make it harder for U-boats to target them from far away.

They wanted to try a technique called camouflage (CAM-uh-flahge), which was adapted for use in the military by artists in France in 1914 and which comes from a French word that means "to disguise." It conceals an object by covering it in a pattern that matches the appearance and color of the background.

Originally, camouflaged objects were covered in browns and greens to match the colors of leaves and the ground. This worked great on land, but when ships were camouflaged in blues and greens to match the colors of the ocean, the ships stood out. The ocean in the background changes color all the time depending on the color of the sky. The Allied navies soon realized that this kind of camouflage wouldn't work on ships.

They considered covering ships in mirrors, disguising them to look like giant whales, or hiding them in canvas to look like floating islands! Thomas Edison, a famous inventor, suggested the floating islands. When he tested the idea out on a ship in New York Harbor, the wind blew the canvas off the ship.

The Allies soon realized that even if a ship itself could somehow be concealed, it was impossible to hide the smoke coming out of its smokestack. They needed to find another way.

Early in the war, a zoologist (zoo-AHL-uh-jist) named John Graham Kerr saw the patterns on zebras and tigers and had an idea for what is called disrupting camouflage. Instead of blending in with the background, this kind of camouflage uses bold lines and colors to disrupt or change the appearance of an object to confuse an enemy. It is similar to how a zebra's stripes make it hard for a lion to see the shape of a single zebra in a herd.

Kerr shared his idea with the British Navy. But no one took it seriously until 1917, when a British man named Norman Wilkinson expanded on it. Wilkinson was an artist known for his realistic paintings of ships, but his idea for camouflaging *real* ships was closer to a new art style called Cubism (CUE-biz-um). Cubist painters like Pablo Picasso and Georges Braque made paintings of objects that looked like they were in fragments. If they made a painting of a guitar, for example, they didn't just paint the curvy outline. Instead, they made it look as if the guitar were broken into pieces by painting dark lines and adding different shades and colors to it.

Wilkinson tested a similar painting style on small ship models. Up close, the bright patterns made ships stand out even *more* than usual, but from far away, they made it harder to figure out the ships' exact outline, shape, and direction.

This colorful camouflage was called Razzle Dazzle painting. It wasn't perfect, but it seemed to decrease the number of torpedo strikes. (Find out more about how it worked later in this book!)

The Allies were eager to use this invention, which they nicknamed "Dazzle" painting, on their ships and other targets. It was a big job, and they needed a lot of painters to make it happen. At that time in the United States, women weren't often encouraged to work, but since many men were busy fighting in the war, women had the chance to contribute. A group of women in New York City formed the Women's Reserve Camouflage Corps. In Union Square, they painted a huge ship with Dazzle painting!

They tested out camouflage outfits called rock suits, which were meant to look like boulders, by hiding in plain sight in Central Park. Their disguises worked so well that the police said that they could only find the camouflaged women in the park if one of them moved by mistake!

Before long there were Dazzle ships, ambulances, and even airplanes. The Dazzle patterns eventually inspired fashion, too, showing up on bathing suits and ball gowns!

Better yet, the work of the Women's Reserve Camouflage Corps and the creativity of the people who invented Dazzle painting helped save Allies' ships and lives.

Chapter 3
The Choctaw Telephone Squad

In World War I, another great idea came about because the Allies had a problem. Time after time, the Germans kept cracking the Allies' secret codes, and the Allies needed a better way to share information among themselves.

It was reported that one day a US Army captain found a solution when he overheard a conversation between two soldiers from the Choctaw tribe. Their language was unlike anything he had ever heard, and he realized it could be used as a code that might be very difficult to figure out.

He asked the soldiers to test the idea. They used a field telephone to send a message spoken entirely in Choctaw from one Choctaw soldier to another.

We don't know what that message said, but we know that the plan worked! The Choctaw soldier on the other end of the telephone line quickly translated the message. Soon eight soldiers became the first members of a top secret Choctaw Telephone Squad. They were sent to different locations in the war zone.

They didn't hesitate to put their lives in danger even though, as children, the US government sent many of them to boarding schools where they were punished for speaking Choctaw instead of English. That was just one of many ways the United States had treated American Indians badly.

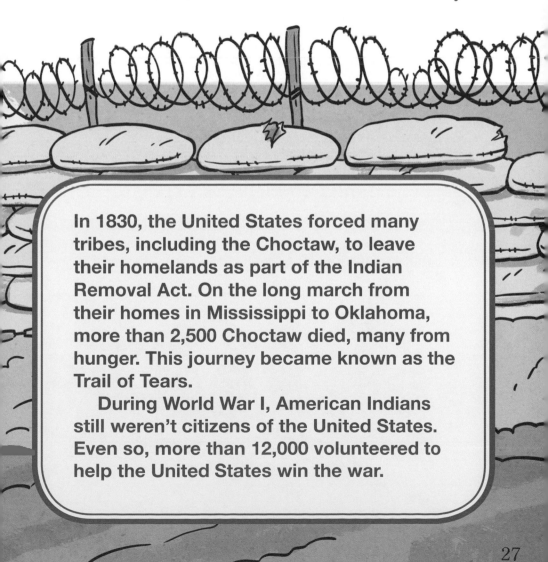

In 1830, the United States forced many tribes, including the Choctaw, to leave their homelands as part of the Indian Removal Act. On the long march from their homes in Mississippi to Oklahoma, more than 2,500 Choctaw died, many from hunger. This journey became known as the Trail of Tears.

During World War I, American Indians still weren't citizens of the United States. Even so, more than 12,000 volunteered to help the United States win the war.

Eventually there were around twenty code talkers, as they are now called. They could send and receive messages more quickly than any coding machine could. This was important because a message received a minute too late could mean many people might get hurt.

Since the Choctaw language didn't include words related to modern war, the code talkers had to be creative. They made up phrases and code words. Instead of "machine gun," they said "little gun shoot fast" in Choctaw. In place of a specific army unit's name, they assigned a coded phrase like "corn grain three."

This system worked better than anyone imagined. The Germans never figured out how to translate Choctaw, which meant that the Allies' secrets remained secret.

It also meant that the United States could use code talkers again in the future. The United States made the Telephone Squad promise to keep their story a secret. When the Second World War began, their work inspired Navajo code talkers and others to send secret messages in their languages, saving countless lives. Without code talkers, the world might look very different today.

In 1924, American Indians were finally given citizenship in the United States, but the Choctaw Telephone Squad wasn't officially recognized for its service until 2008, when the Code Talkers Recognition Act was passed. The original Choctaw code talkers didn't live to see that day, or receive the medals made in their honor, but their contribution will never be forgotten.

Chapter 4
Eugene Bullard:
The Fearless Flyer

World War I was the first war fought with airplanes, and many people wanted to learn to fly, including a man named Eugene Bullard. He was the first African American fighter pilot in the world, but he never was allowed to fly for the US Air Force.

Bullard was born in Georgia in 1895, and his father had been enslaved. Even though slavery had been abolished in 1865, African Americans did not have the same rights as other people in the United States.

When he was sixteen years old, Bullard wanted to find a place to live that was free of the racism he had experienced in the United States. He snuck on board a freight ship and sailed to Europe.

First, he made his way to London and earned a living as a boxer and performer.

In 1913, Bullard traveled to Paris, France,

for a boxing match. He felt accepted and at home in that country, so he decided to move there.

When World War I began in 1914, Bullard joined the French Foreign Legion, a unit made up of people from foreign countries. As a soldier, he was badly wounded in the Battle of Verdun in 1916. While he recovered, Bullard made a daring move. He bet a friend $2,000 that he could enlist in the French flying service as a pilot.

Bullard won that bet and began flight training! He flew in more than twenty battles and was later honored fifteen times for his service by the French government.

When the United States joined the Allied forces in 1917, Bullard wanted to join the US Air Force and fight for his country, but he was rejected.

He was told it was because his rank in France was lower than the rank required in the US Air Force. The truth was, he was rejected because of racism. The US Air Force would not allow African Americans to be pilots.

After the war he went on to own a nightclub in France and spend time with legendary writers like F. Scott Fitzgerald and performers like Josephine Baker. He even became a spy during World War II, but when he found out his life was in danger, he had to flee.

Bullard returned to the United States, where he worked a variety of jobs, from unloading ships to operating elevators at the iconic Rockefeller Center. He was sad to find he was still experiencing racism, and he became active in the civil rights movement.

Bullard didn't have an easy life, but he pursued his dreams, and eventually the US Air Force realized it had been wrong to not let him fly. In 1994, years after his death, they made him a second lieutenant to honor his service. Bullard and his accomplishments are celebrated in museums across the country.

When World War I ended in 1918, some thought it would be "the war to end all wars." It had caused so much destruction that countries didn't want to let war happen again, but peace only lasted a short time. The Second World War caused even more devastation.

Even so, the positive things that started in the First World War only grew. Women in the Women's Reserve Camouflage Corps didn't have the right to vote, but that changed in 1920. The Choctaw code talkers weren't citizens of the United States, but that changed in 1924. Eugene Bullard couldn't fly for the US Air Force, but he helped pave the way for African American pilots to fly in World War II. Their bravery helped change the world for the better.

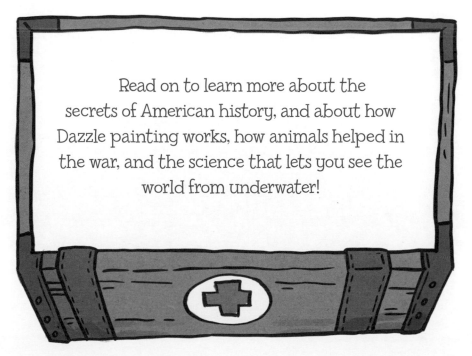

Read on to learn more about the secrets of American history, and about how Dazzle painting works, how animals helped in the war, and the science that lets you see the world from underwater!

How Dazzle Painting Works

Dazzle painting looked pretty cool, but it also served a purpose. The goal was to confuse the people aiming torpedoes at Allied ships. This was possible because of how submarine torpedoes worked in World War I: they had to be aimed at wherever a ship was *headed*, rather than at its current location. People on the submarine had just seconds to guess where a ship was going based on a series of clues.

Direction: To figure out a ship's direction, they looked at the angle of the ship and of its smokestack.

Speed: To help determine its speed, they observed the height of the waves hitting the front of the ship. A slow-moving ship creates a smaller wave than a fast-moving ship.

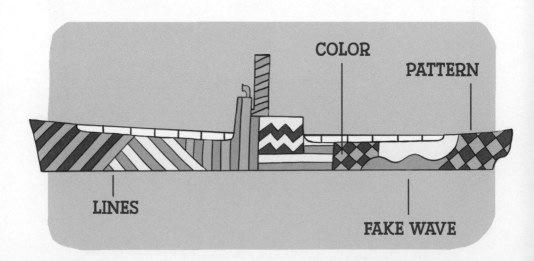

COLOR

PATTERN

LINES

FAKE WAVE

Razzle Dazzle It!

On a Dazzle ship, the camouflage disrupted the ship's appearance.

Pattern and Color: The overall pattern and many colors of Dazzle painting made it harder to determine a ship's shape and outline from far away.

Lines: A curved, dark line painted on the bottom of a ship and angled lines painted on the smokestack made it appear to be headed in a different direction than its actual course.

A Fake Wave: A fake wave painted near the middle of a ship made it appear to be moving faster or slower than it really was, and made it seem like the middle of the ship was actually the *front* of the ship.

All these things confused the people aiming the torpedoes into thinking a ship was traveling faster or slower, or at a different angle than it really was. Sometimes, it made them shoot the torpedo at the wrong location. Mission accomplished!

What would you Dazzle if you could? Ask a grown-up to help you find an object to paint in a Dazzle painting style, or use colored pencils or crayons on a separate piece of paper to make up your own Dazzle pattern!

Animal Heroes

Did you know that more than sixteen million animals were deployed in World War I? Horses and mules transported soldiers and supplies. Some even carried secret plans and messages. Pigeons flew great lengths, often across battlefields, to carry messages,  while dogs moved between the trenches to pass along important communications. Here is the story of one unlikely animal hero who saved lives!

A Dear Friend: Cher Ami was a pigeon whose name means "dear friend" in French. From 1917 to 1918, Cher Ami delivered messages among US outposts in France. In 1918 a group of two hundred American soldiers found themselves trapped. They were separated from other troops, stuck at the bottom of a hill, and surrounded by the German Army. All hope seemed lost, especially when other American forces mistook them for

Germans and started firing at them! Their leader, Major Charles Whittlesey, twice attempted to send a message by carrier pigeon, but both birds were shot down.

Then it was Cher Ami's turn. Bullets flew at him the entire twenty-five miles he traveled back to the Allies. He was badly injured on the journey. Still, he arrived with Whittlesey's message: "We are along the road parallel 276.4. Our artillery is dropping a barrage directly on us. For heaven's sake stop it." Thanks to Cher Ami, the Allies stopped firing at Whittlesey and his men, and they managed to make their way out of German territory. Cher Ami was a hero!

The Scoop on Periscopes

During World War I, the technology that people on submarines used to detect enemy ships from underwater didn't work very well. Instead, to see above the water's surface without being noticed, people used a cool device called a **periscope** (PEAR-uh-scope). It can be raised up out of the water to help people see the view from down below.

How It Works

A periscope is a long tube that has openings on opposite sides and is fitted with two mirrors. Some periscopes also include lenses that magnify, or enlarge, the image seen through them. In a simple periscope, one mirror is placed at the top of the tube, across from the opening, and another at the bottom.

For a periscope to work, the mirrors must be facing each other and also be **parallel** (PEAR-uh-lell), or placed at the same angle. This needs to be a 45-degree angle, or exactly halfway between horizontal and vertical. **Horizontal** (HOR-i-zon-tuhl) is another word for the flat, side-to-side angle of the sky's horizon. **Vertical** (VER-tih-cuhl) is another word for the straight-up-and-down angle of a flagpole.

When light travels through the top opening of a periscope and hits the top mirror, the angle of the

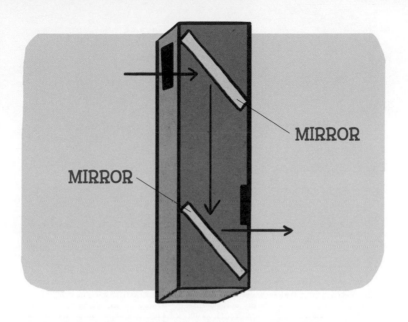

mirror helps bounce the light down through the tube to the lower mirror. The angle of the lower mirror helps bounce the light out through the bottom opening and into a viewer's eye . . . so he or she can see the world from underwater!

Periscopes weren't just used on submarines in World War I. They were also used to help people fighting in trenches see the view up top from down below!

TAKE THE FEARLESS FLYERS, DAZZLE PAINTERS, AND CODE TALKERS! QUIZ

1. What year did World War I begin?

a. 2014   b. 1905   c. 1914

2. What does "camouflage" mean?

a. to uncover   b. to disguise   c. to make bigger

3. Which American Indian language was used to decode messages during World War I?

a. Navajo   b. Choctaw   c. Cree

4. How many American Indians volunteered in World War I?

a. more than 12,000   b. less than 300   c. more than 4,000

5. What originally brought Eugene Bullard to Paris in 1914?

a. he made a bet   b. he attended a concert   c. he participated in a
                                                         boxing match

6. How did a fake wave painted on the middle of a Dazzle ship fool the enemy?

a. the ship appeared to be moving faster or slower than it really was

b. the ship appeared to be sinking

c. the ship appeared to be on fire

7. What kind of bird was Cher Ami?

a. pigeon   b. dove   c. eagle

8. How many mirrors are found in a simple periscope?

a. four   b. ten   c. two

Answers: 1.c 2.b 3.b 4.a 5.c 6.a 7.a 8.c